Prentice Hall
LITERATURE
Timeless Voices, Timeless Themes

Extension Activities

Prentice Hall

Upper Saddle River, New Jersey
Glenview, Illinois
Needham, Massachusetts

ISBN 0-13-062390-3

2 3 4 5 6 7 8 9 10   05 04 03 02

CONTENTS

UNIT 1: INDEPENDENCE AND IDENTITY

UNIT 2: COMMON THREADS

UNIT 3: WHAT MATTERS

UNIT 4: RESOLVING CONFLICTS

UNIT 5: JUST FOR FUN

UNIT 6: SHORT STORIES

UNIT 7: NONFICTION

UNIT 8: DRAMA

UNIT 9: POETRY

UNIT 10: MYTHS, LEGENDS, AND FOLK TALES

"The Cat Who Thought She Was a Dog and the Dog Who Thought He Was a Cat"
by Isaac Bashevis Singer

Extension Activities

1. **Storyboard** Pretend that a television producer is interested in turning "The Cat Who Thought She Was a Dog and the Dog Who Thought He Was a Cat" into a cartoon. You have been asked to create the storyboard, or a series of boxes in which you draw the major actions of the story. You can use stick figures to indicate people and their actions. Write a short description of the scene under each picture.

2. **Role Play** With a partner, role-play a dialogue between Jan Skiva and the priest. Assume Jan has not yet returned the mirror. One of you should take the part of Jan who describes life before and after buying the mirror. The other should play the part of the priest who offers Jan advice.

3. **Character Map** Create a character map for each of the characters in the fable. Examine the fable closely for details, including each character's traits as well as the characters' relationships to each other. Use your character map to draw conclusions about the fable's lesson about human behavior. Explain your character map to your classmates.

4. **Essay on Mirrors** Mirrors figure prominently throughout fiction. The wicked queen in "Snow White and the Seven Dwarfs" consults her reflection in a mirror to find out who is the fairest in the land. Alice in Lewis Carroll's *Through the Looking Glass* finds a new world behind a mirror. Why do you think this is true? What might a mirror stand for? Write a brief essay in which you consider the significance of the mirror in fiction.

5. **Fable** Write a fable featuring Burek and Kot in which the animals speak and act like humans. Conclude your fable with a brief moral, drawn from their experience, that teaches a practical lesson about life.

6. **Dual Portrait** The women in this story do not find fault with their appearance until they see themselves reflected in the mirror. Choose one of the women and draw a picture of her as she imagined she looked before she sees her reflection. Then draw her as she views herself in the mirror. Base your drawings on details from the selection.

7. **Television News Team** In this selection, a mirror causes problems for characters who did not own one before. Imagine how the sudden introduction of a common object such as a telephone or an electric lamp might affect a family or community. With a partner, brainstorm the conflicts that might result. Then, play the parts of a television news team. One of you should "report live" from the scene, while the other plays the part of the news anchor who asks the reporter questions about the problem. Rehearse your scene and then present it to the class.

Extension Activities

1. **Helpful Hints** In "Two Kinds," Mr. Chong shows Jing-mei ways to improve her piano playing. Choose an activity in which you are skilled. It can be a sport, hobby, or other interest. Write a short list of tips on how others can become skilled in your activity.

2. **Journal Entry** Write a journal entry from the point of view of a girl or boy your age who is pushed to excel by a friend or family member. Relate an incident that occurs on the day of the entry and how you imagine the child feels about it. The incident may be a positive experience, such as a boy hitting his first home run after his father has helped him correct his swing.

3. **Rewrite** Rewrite the story as it might have unfolded had Jing-mei excelled when her mother first began testing her abilities. Would Jing-mei have continued to try to be a prodigy? How would the relationship with her mother have developed as they pursued this shared goal?

4. **Report on China** Conduct research about the conditions for women in China in 1949. For example, were women allowed to own property, hold jobs, choose their husbands, or participate in government? How might the United States have seemed, by contrast, a land of unlimited opportunity? Summarize your findings in a brief written report.

5. **Training Manual** With a group of classmates, create a lighthearted training manual for parents: How to Raise the Perfect Child, How to Create an Instant Prodigy, or How to Rear a Genius. Brainstorm for specific strategies and examples as well as for ways to organize your manual.

6. **Mirror Images** What do you see when you look in the mirror? Do you see the same person as your friends and family see? Jing-mei saw a split image of herself—the ordinary child who disappointed her mother and the prodigy who was powerful and willful. Paint or draw the two sides of yourself as you understand them.

7. **Concert** Among the pieces of music mentioned in this selection are "Pleading Child" and "Perfectly Contented" from Robert Schumann's *Scenes from Childhood*. Obtain recordings of these pieces from your school or local library, and play them for the class. Then lead a class discussion about how each piece of music reflects its title.

from *Song of Myself* by Walt Whitman

"I'm Nobody" by Emily Dickinson

"Me" by Walter de la Mare

Extension Activities

1. **Read Aloud and Paraphrase** With a partner, take turns reading the poems aloud. Read two lines of each poem at a time. Look up any words you do not know in a dictionary. After each turn, tell your partner in a sentence or two what the poet expressed in the lines you read.

2. **Poem About Somebody** Imagine a person the opposite of Emily Dickinson—someone who likes being "Somebody." You may choose someone you know personally, a favorite celebrity, or someone from your imagination. Write a poem about the person's need to be famous and important.

3. **Film Outline** Conduct research about the life of Dickinson, de la Mare, or Whitman to find out more about the self the poet describes in his or her poem. After completing your research, write an outline for a film about the poet's life. Select several poems or stanzas of poems from among the poet's works to present at appropriate points in the film.

4. **Journal Entry** Imagine that Emily Dickinson published her poems and achieved fame during her lifetime. How would she have reacted to the public attention? Write a journal entry from her point of view after a day of particularly high public visibility. Describe her feelings and any internal conflict she may have experienced.

5. **Role Play** Imagine that Dickinson and Whitman appear on a television talk show to discuss the topic: Being Yourself. Dickinson has read *Song of Myself* and Whitman has read "I'm Nobody." With a partner, act out what the poets say about each other's poems and the topic of being yourself. First jot down ideas based on your understanding of the poems. Then role-play the talk show discussion for the class.

6. **Collage** With a small group of classmates, create a "being oneself" collage. Search magazines and newspapers for photos of people expressing themselves in a unique way. Include people of different ages, ethnic backgrounds, and genders in different countries and locations. For example, you might show workers on a Costa Rican plantation or a sunbather on a Spanish beach. Display the collage in the classroom.

7. **Music for Poetry** The poems *Song of Myself*, "I'm Nobody," and "Me" all address the topic of identity, but each expresses different feelings and uses different poetic rhythms. Select a piece of music to accompany each poem. Match the rhythm and feelings of the music to the rhythm and feelings of the poem. Play the selected pieces for the class. Challenge classmates to guess which piece of music goes with which poem.

Extension Activities

1. **Sequence Events** In "My Furthest-Back Person," Haley relates events that took place shortly before the selection was written, events that took place centuries ago, and events that took place when he was a boy. Read the selection with a partner, and list the events in the order in which they occur. You need not use complete sentences or write a full description of the event. For example, you may just write: Kinte captured.

2. **Role Play** Think about the reactions of Kinte's relatives and friends when he did not return from cutting wood for his drum. Did they know about the slave traders? Would they expect him to have died in a fatal accident in the jungle? With a partner, role-play a dialogue between two of Kinte's relatives when he fails to return. Have them imagine what might have happened to him and suggest a plan to find him.

3. **Africa's Changing Face** Some of the countries Haley visited have changed several times since Kinte was captured. Boundaries have been redrawn, and country names have changed. Using on-line or library sources, study the history of West Africa since Kinte landed in Annapolis. Create a series of outline maps, showing the boundaries and names of West African countries or regions since 1767. Write a brief chronology to accompany the maps. Then make a presentation to the class.

4. **Book Proposal** In the world of publishing, a book proposal includes a description of the author's purpose, the book's main idea, and a brief outline of the content. Imagine you are Haley returning to the United States from the village of the Kinte clan. Write a book proposal for "My Furthest-Back Person."

5. **Map** Haley names many places in "My Furthest-Back Person." Several are places he visited in Africa in his search for Kinte's place of birth, and one is the place Kinte landed when he was taken from Africa. On an outline map of the world, show the countries Haley visited. Locate the places he names. Trace his route from where he first landed in Africa to the village where he found his roots. Locate and mark the city in the United States where Kinte first landed as a slave.

6. **Interview** Imagine that Haley has just returned from the village where Kinte was born. With a group of classmates, stage a television interview of Haley. Assign the roles of Haley and the news reporters. Agree on a list of questions for the reporters to ask as they interview Haley about his experience. After a rehearsal, conduct the interview before the class. You may wish to tape the interview and play it for another class.

7. **Pantomime** Read Haley's account of the villagers' behavior as they become aware that Haley is descended from Kunta Kinte. Imagine details of your own. With a group of classmates, use gestures but not words to dramatize the events from the moment the griot recognizes Haley as Kunta Kinte's descendant to the point where Haley gathers with his relatives for a photo.

"The Third Level" by Jack Finney

Extension Activities

1. **Retelling** Imagine you work for a film producer and your job is to find stories that will make hit movies. You think "The Third Level" will make a great film. In a brief outline, retell the story for the benefit of the producer. List the events in the order the audience will view them. To keep the time sequence clear, circle the events that take place in 1894.

2. **Drawing—Past and Present** Finney provides a description of the third level subway station in 1894. Either from your own knowledge or from photos, draw a scene of present-day Grand Central Station. Then draw the third level station from Finney's description. Post your drawings in the classroom.

3. **Oral Report** To live in the world of 1894 Sam needed to manage without the many modern conveniences he had grown used to before he traveled back in time. Using periodicals or on-line sources, conduct research about devices invented between 1894 and 1940. Select at least five items. Present an oral report to the class explaining how these devices changed people's lives and what adjustments Sam needed to make to live without them.

4. **Science Fiction Story** Write your own science fiction story about a person who travels forward or backward in time. Imagine how the person must adjust to unfamiliar technology, customs, and pace of life. Decide whether the character will return to the present. If the character stays in the new time, will he or she be happy about the change? Circulate your story for your classmates to read.

5. **Journal Entry** Sam longed for the simpler life of the past. However, he probably needed to make some major adjustments to the people, customs, and lack of conveniences. Write a journal entry in which Sam describes his feelings about living in 1894. What might he miss about his old life in modern time? What pleasant or unpleasant surprises may have greeted him in the past? Have him examine both the positive and negative effects of the change he made.

6. **Collage** Work with a group to create a "then and now" collage contrasting scenes in small towns at the turn of the century with those of modern-day New York. Search magazines and newspapers for present-day scenes. For turn-of-the-century pictures, you may need to photocopy paintings or photos from books about the period. Display the collage in the classroom.

7. **Role Play** Imagine the reactions of Sam's office staff and patients when he disappears. With three classmates, role-play a scene at Sam's office after he has been missing for three days. Assign the roles of two of the office staff, Charlie, and another patient. How long would it take the staff and patients to realize he was gone? How would they go about looking for him? Would his staff be able to keep the office open? For how long?

Extension Activities

1. **Paragraph** The boy's father tries to comfort him by reading aloud from a book about pirates. Suppose that you are sick in bed for a few days. Write a paragraph or two telling the kinds of activities you would choose in order to keep occupied. Would you read books and magazines, watch television, listen to music, or draw pictures? Explain how any of these choices would help to take your mind off the unpleasantness of being ill.

2. **Oral Report** The father uses a German nickname for his son, and the boy has been to school in France. If you had a chance to attend school for a year in a foreign country, where would you like to go? Choose a country, and then use library or Internet resources to find out more about its language and culture. Present your results in an illustrated oral report to the class.

3. **Journal Entries** We learn very little from the story about the father's thoughts and inner feelings. Write a series of journal entries in which you record the father's reactions to his conversations with his son, the doctor's visit, and the quail-hunting excursion.

4. **Plot Analysis** In a paragraph or two, analyze what the quail-hunting episode contributes to the story. Why do you think Hemingway included it? Consider how the episode may help to develop characterization, setting, and mood.

5. **Metric Chart** Most countries in the world use the metric system of weights (such as grams and kilograms) and measures (such as meters and kilometers). Working in a small group, draw a chart that shows frequently used metric units, the abbreviations for these units, and their equivalents in the English system. You can round off equivalents where necessary: for example, 1 kg = 2.2 lb.

6. **Anecdote** Suppose the events in the story actually happened to you when you were a child. Tell the story as a humorous anecdote to amuse your friends. After rehearsing your narrative a few times, try it out on a small group of classmates.

7. **Illustrations** The story contains a number of clues to the setting. Work with a small group and plan two illustrations for the story. Which scenes and characters will you show? What will be the mood of your illustrations? Create the illustrations using watercolors, markers, or another medium of your choice.

"**Was Tarzan a Three-Bandage Man?**" by Bill Cosby

"**Oranges**" by Gary Soto

Extension Activities

1. **Story** Rewrite "Oranges" as a short story, using the same first-person point of view that Soto uses in the poem. Create dialogue and names for the characters. Include vivid sensory details appropriate for the setting and mood.

2. **Paragraph** Cosby mentions his boyhood heroes in baseball, football, and boxing. Write a paragraph or two telling about someone you admire in professional sports, or in another field, such as music. Explain why you admire this person and what you have learned from watching the person perform.

3. **Letter** At the end of this story, Cosby admits that he and his friends were idolizing the wrong people. Write a letter to Fat Albert, Junior, and Eddie telling them politely that they picked the wrong heroes. Suggest people they might have looked up to instead.

4. **Round-Table Discussion** With a small group of classmates, conduct a round-table discussion about a current sports issue, such as big-money contracts or athletes as role models. Use the school or local library to find an editorial or letter to the editor expressing views on a certain sports issue. Base your discussion on why you agree or disagree with the writer.

5. **Book Jacket** Design and create a book jacket for a biography of a person you admire. You may draw a design or use a copy of a photograph, drawing, or painting. You may wish to include some quotations from celebrities or experts in a particular field. Think of a suitable title for the book. Include some information (you may make it up) for the back of your book jacket. When you are finished, display it for the class.

6. **Personal Narrative** Write a brief personal narrative, telling about a time when you suddenly realized something important about yourself. Use chronological order, and include details of your thoughts and feelings.

7. **Imitation** Think of someone you admire. Does that person have a particular way of walking or using hand gestures? Practice imitating the particular way that this person does something. How does it make you feel to imitate this person? What do you think these motions and gestures reveal about the person?

Extension Activities

1. **Oral Report** The Smithsonian Institution in Washington, D.C., has been called the nation's attic. Use library resources or the Internet to find out more about the different museums that make up the Smithsonian. Sum up your findings in an oral report to the class.

2. **Holiday Menu** Does your family have some favorite times for get-togethers, such as holidays, birthdays, or anniversaries? Plan a special meal for a family reunion. For your menu, choose foods that are representative of your ethnic heritage or characteristic of your region of the country. Then write a paragraph or two explaining the significance of the dishes you have chosen.

3. **Tribute Poem** Use the poem in the selection as a model for your own tribute poem to a family member, friend, or role model. Your poem may or may not rhyme, and the lengths of the lines may vary. Include vivid images that appeal to some of the five senses: sight, hearing, taste, smell, and touch.

4. **Research Report** Research the life and works of Phillis Wheatley. Find a copy of her poem "To His Excellency General Washington," which was written soon after the start of the American Revolution. This poem, like the one Alice Walker wrote for her mother, is in the form of a tribute. Write a brief report in which you sum up the results of your research and your reactions to Wheatley's poem.

5. **Interview and Paragraph** The author says that one way her mother expressed creativity was through storytelling. In an interview, ask an older family member or friend to tell a story about an experience that happened before you were born. Make notes on the story, and then write a summary in a paragraph or two.

6. **Oral Performance** Rehearse an oral interpretation of the poem in the selection, or choose another poem with a similar subject and theme for oral performance. Pay special attention to sound effects, volume, pitch, pacing, and emphasis. Then perform the poem for a small group of classmates.

7. **A Letter to the Author** Write a letter to the author in which you tell her your reactions to "In Search of Our Mothers' Gardens." Be specific about the parts of the essay you like best, and include any questions you may have.

Extension Activities

1. **Round Table Discussion** Join with a small group of classmates and organize a round table discussion on the different verbal and nonverbal ways we try to make impressions on others.

2. **Country Profile** "Melting Pot" refers to a number of foreign countries, such as Ecuador, Ireland, Italy, and Yugoslavia. Choose one of the countries mentioned that interests you. Using an almanac, atlas, encyclopedia, or other reference book, find out basic information about this country, such as population, language spoken, major cities, and so forth. Then write a "country profile" in which you report your results.

3. **Documentary** With a small group of classmates, research Ellis Island in New York Harbor, which was the arrival station for millions of immigrants to the United States. Find some photos or video of this historic site, which is now a national monument. Use your findings to create a short documentary report.

4. **Editorial** Should students in Grades 7–12 be required to take a foreign language? Write an editorial for your school newspaper giving your opinion. Be sure to support your view with specific facts, reasons, and examples.

5. **Photo Essay** A photo essay uses a sequence of carefully chosen photographs, together with brief captions, to tell a story. Working with a small group, create a photo essay about a place in your community, such as your school, neighborhood, local park, hospital, or museum. Take your own photographs, or use pictures from brochures or old newspapers and magazines.

6. **Dialogue** With a partner, create a dialogue that might happen between Victor and Teresa six months after the action of "Seventh Grade." Rehearse your dialogue, and then role-play the encounter for an audience of your classmates.

7. **Interview and Paragraph** In "Melting Pot, the author writes, "Change comes hard in America. . ." Interview an older person in your neighborhood to find out how much the surroundings have changed in the last thirty years. Also find out if this person agrees with the author's statement about change. Summarize the results of your interview in a paragraph or two.

Unit 2: Common Threads

Extension Activities

1. **Fable** Find out more about the ancient Greek writer Aesop. Choose one of Aesop's famous fables, identify the moral or lesson, and then read the fable aloud to a small group of your classmates.

2. **Poll** In a recent poll in England, Rudyard Kipling's "If—" was voted the most popular poem ever written by a British author. Make a list of a dozen or so well-known poems or songs. You might include some of the poems in this textbook. Then poll your classmates to find out their three favorites.

3. **Research Report** Law enforcement agencies now use DNA analysis as well as fingerprints to identify individuals. Find out more about this technique. What is DNA? What methods are used in this kind of analysis and how accurate are they? Sum up your results in a brief oral report.

4. **Poem** Write a poem about your own hopes for the future. Use the form of Kipling's poem "If—" as a springboard. For example, you could repeat a word like *when* or *someday* at the beginning of each line or set of lines. Your poem may or may not rhyme.

5. **Film Review** Rudyard Kipling was born in India and wrote many adventure stories about the Indian jungle. Locate the film entitled *Rudyard Kipling's Jungle Book* (1994), which was based on some of Kipling's most famous stories. Watch the film, and then write a short review in which you evaluate it in terms of the story, characters, and element of suspense.

6. **Humorous Dialogue** With a partner, create a humorous dialogue between two speakers, one of whom is very large (such as a whale) and one of whom is very small (such as an ant). Rehearse your dialogue, and then perform it for a group of your classmates.

7. **Music Album** What songs or musical pieces best express your individual personality? Make a list of your favorite musical selections. Then find some recordings and compile an anthology on audiocassette. Play some of your favorites for an audience of family members or classmates.

"Mother to Son" by Langston Hughes
"The Courage That My Mother Had" by Edna St. Vincent Millay
"The Hummingbird That Lived Through Winter" by William Saroyan

Extension Activities

1. **Metaphors** Good metaphors are fresh, effective comparisons between two unlike things. Saying that life isn't a crystal stair, for example, is fresher and more vivid than saying that life isn't a bowl of cherries. Make up fresh metaphors for the following nouns, using *is* or *is not* to connect each noun with a metaphorical word or phrase: courage, honesty, sympathy, encouragement, respect.

2. **Field Guide Entry** William Saroyan vividly describes the hummingbird. Choose one of your favorite birds or other animals and write a field guide entry. Give a detailed physical description, and note where and when the bird or animal can best be seen.

3. **Character Sketch** Dikran in "The Hummingbird That Lived Through Winter" can be described as a mentor, or someone who helps and guides someone else. In one or two paragraphs, write a character sketch of an older relative or neighbor whom you respect for his or her wisdom or achievement.

4. **Round Table Discussion** With a small group of classmates, organize a round table discussion. Share ideas about which of the selections you like best. Support your opinions with reasons and specific references to the selections.

5. **Report on Animal Symbolism** In many cultures, animals are regarded as symbolic of certain human qualities. For example, a lion often symbolizes royalty, while a fox may symbolize cunning. Choose an animal and research the symbolism that has grown up around it in folk tales, poetry, painting, or sculpture. Report your findings in a brief illustrated oral report.

6. **Human Interest Story** These selections stress the importance of never giving up. Write a human interest feature for a newspaper or magazine that focuses on the importance of persistence and determination. You can use an example from personal experience, or you can draw on the experience of someone you know or have read about.

7. **Scene** With a partner, create and perform a scene between the mother and son in "Mother to Son." First discuss what might have motivated the mother to deliver this speech to her son. Is he discouraged about something? Has he asked her for advice? Has he done something she disapproves of? Based on your answers to these questions, write the scene between the mother and the son that preceded the poem. Practice the scene and then perform it for your class.

Extension Activities

1. **Prologue** How did the King of the Forest get into such a jam that he had to be rescued by Mr. Peters? Write a short prologue, or introduction, to the story, explaining what the king was doing and giving details about his ability to change his form.

2. **Explanation** Why is the choice of a swan appropriate for the character of Leita? In a paragraph, explain the characteristics associated with swans that make this bird suitable for the fairy tale.

3. **Report** Scientists identify every living organism by a two-part scientific name that often uses words from Latin or Greek. For example, the Trumpeter Swan is *Cygnus buccinator*. Use a dictionary or encyclopedia to find out more about Linnaeus, the eighteenth-century Swedish scientist who invented this system. Then find examples of scientific names for other animals. Present your findings in a brief written report.

4. **Summary** Another famous story on the theme of three wishes is "The Monkey's Paw" by W. W. Jacobs (1863–1943). Find a copy of this classic horror story and read the tale. Then summarize the story orally for a small group of your classmates. Point out two similarities and two differences between "The Monkey's Paw" and "The Third Wish."

5. **Illustration** Working in a small group, draw a picture illustrating one of the following characters: Leita, Mr. Peters, or the King of the Forest. Place your character in a setting that is appropriate for her or his personality and actions during the story.

6. **Prose Poem** A prose poem is a short, personal composition in prose that has many of the devices of poetry, such as strong rhythm, vivid imagery, and striking figures of speech like similes or metaphors. Suppose that you, like Mr. Peters, have three wishes. Write a prose poem telling about your choices and the reasons for them.

7. **Paragraph** Find out more about the story of Swan Lake, a famous ballet by the Russian composer Peter Ilyich Tchaikovsky. Listen to some of the music from this ballet, and then write a paragraph describing your reactions to it.

Extension Activities

1. **Paragraph** Have you ever pressed your physical limits the way Rudi does in "A Boy and a Man"? Write a paragraph about a time that you or someone you know "pushed the envelope" or went all out to achieve an objective.

2. **Country Report** These accounts of mountaineering take place in two small countries in Europe and Asia: Switzerland and Nepal, respectively. Choose one of these countries, and use almanacs, atlases, magazines, or Internet resources to find out more about its geography, climate, population, language, and other factual details. Sum up your results in a written report.

3. **News Article** The first mountaineers to conquer the summit of Mount Everest were Sir Edmund Hillary of New Zealand and Tenzing Norkay of Nepal. Find out more about their landmark expedition in 1953. Then summarize your results in a news article.

4. **Inventory** What kind of clothing and what sorts of tools do modern mountaineers need? Use sports magazines, encyclopedias, and Internet resources to find out. Then make an inventory or detailed list of the equipment you would need if you went mountain climbing.

5. **Magazine Article** Explorers and mountaineers have often been the subjects of beautifully illustrated articles in *National Geographic*. Scan some past issues of this magazine, and find an illustrated article that appeals to you. Read the article, take notes, and then summarize the article orally for a small group of your classmates.

6. **Science Report** What kinds of animals, birds, and other organisms can live at extremely high altitudes? What special adaptations do these creatures possess in order to deal with cold temperatures, thin air, and scarce food? Use reference books and Internet resources to find out, and then write a short report to summarize your results.

7. **Collage** Beginning in very ancient times, mountains have often been featured in the mythology and religious rituals of various cultures. Working with a small group of classmates, find out more about mythological or sacred mountains throughout the world. Using photographs from old issues of magazines or creating your own drawings, assemble a collage that shows several of these mountains.

Unit 3: What Matters

"The Charge of the Light Brigade" by Alfred, Lord Tennyson
"The Enemy" by Alice Walker
from Henry V by William Shakespeare

Extension Activities

1. **Paragraph** What does Tennyson's use of rhythm and repetition add to "The Charge of the Light Brigade"? Read the poem aloud several times, and make notes on the use of these two techniques. Then write a paragraph explaining how you think rhythm and repetition contribute to the poem's total effect.

2. **Pep Talk** In Shakespeare's play, King Henry V delivers his speech to his soldiers just before an important battle. Write a pep talk for one of the athletic teams at your school just before an important contest or match. Assume that the pep talk will be delivered by a coach or by a team captain.

3. **History Lesson** The Battle of Agincourt, fought in northern France in 1415, is remembered not only because of Shakespeare's *Henry V*. In this battle, the use of longbows by Henry's soldiers changed the way wars were fought. Find out about another landmark battle, such as The Battle of Waterloo in the Napoleonic War or the Battle of Coral Sea in World War II. In an oral report, tell the class why the battle was significant.

4. **Advertising Copy** Judging from Henry in Shakespeare's *Henry V*, what traits were important for a fifteenth-century king? Write a newspaper advertisement for a king. Describe a test the applicant will have to pass, and give your ad the right flavor by imitating the language of the excerpt from *Henry V*.

5. **Biographical Sketch** The British nurse Florence Nightingale (1820–1910) organized a group of thirty-eight women nurses for the Crimean War in 1854. She is regarded as the founder of modern nursing. Find out more about her, and summarize your results in a brief biographical sketch.

6. **Song Festival** Since ancient times, soldiers have sung favorite songs to pass the time, to encourage each other, or to express their longing for home and loved ones. Join with a small group, and choose one of the following conflicts: the American Revolution, the Civil War, or the Vietnam War. Find out which songs were popular among the troops. Then prepare an illustrated report on these songs, including excerpts on audiocassette if possible.

7. **Internet Oral Report** Use the Internet to find out more about poetry slams and contests. What are some of the reasons why so many Americans are reading, reciting, and writing poetry today? Summarize your results in a brief oral report to the class.

"The Californian's Tale" by Mark Twain

"Valediction" by Seamus Heaney

Extension Activities

1. **Letter** Write a letter to Mark Twain. In your letter, tell the author your opinion of the plot and the characters in "The Californian's Tale." Also tell him what you think of the way he described the setting and created suspense. Remember to be as specific as possible.

2. **Dialogue** Write a short dialogue between Henry and his wife in "The Californian's Tale" that might have taken place during the short time they were married. Be sure to make your dialogue consistent with the facts that are given in the story.

3. **Poem** Assume that you are a prospector during the California Gold Rush. Use information in "The Californian's Tale" as a springboard to write a poem in which you, as the speaker, express your thoughts and feelings about your experiences. In your poem, include vivid imagery that appeals to some of the five senses.

4. **Biographical Sketch** Mark Twain's contemporary and rival, Bret Harte, became the best-paid writer in America during the 1870s for his stories about the American West. Use library or Internet resources to find out more about Harte. Then write a paragraph or two in which you give a biographical sketch of this author.

5. **Party Music** Toward the end of Twain's story, the three miners play some music for the party. What is your favorite type of music for a party? Choose two or three selections. Then write a paragraph explaining why you think your group of musical numbers is suitable for a party.

6. **Art History** During the 1860s and 1870s, the leading landscape painter of the American West was a German immigrant named Albert Bierstadt. Together with a small group, find out more about Bierstadt's paintings of the West. Then present an illustrated report to the class as a whole.

7. **Poem** How might the woman who is addressed in "Valediction" respond in a poem of her own? Write a short poem in which the woman is the speaker. In your poem you might explain how or why you "left the house." You might also share your emotions about the separation. Try to include at least two striking, fresh figures of speech in your poem.

Unit 3: What Matters

"Stopping by Woods on a Snowy Evening" by Robert Frost

"Four Skinny Trees" by Sandra Cisneros

"Miracles" by Walt Whitman

Extension Activities

1. **Paragraph** Study carefully the lines of "Stopping by Woods on a Snowy Evening." In a paragraph, explain how the rhyming words at the end of the lines connect the stanzas together. Also tell why you think the final two lines of the last stanza are the same.

2. **Round-Table Discussion** "Miracles" encourages you to think about the meaning of the word *miracle* in a fresh, new way. Together with a small group of classmates, organize a round-table discussion in which you try to develop a new slant or have some unexpected insights on one of the following nouns: *athlete, growth, health, courage, family, happiness,* or *poetry.*

3. **Oral Report** Find out more about the honorary position of Poet Laureate of the United States. When was this job created? Who appoints the Poet Laureate? Who are some of the American poets who have held this position? Share your results in a brief oral report.

4. **Personification** In "Four Skinny Trees," the speaker personifies the trees, or gives them human characteristics. Choose some feature or object in your environment and write either a short paragraph or free-verse poem in which you personify it. Which human qualities or personality traits does this feature of your environment prompt you to think about?

5. **Multimedia Presentation Plan** Assume that you are giving a dramatic reading of Whitman's "Miracles" as part of a multimedia presentation. Which of Whitman's lines would be the most effective basis for visuals? What kind of music would you play in the background? Together with a small group of classmates, develop a plan for a multimedia presentation, focusing on the poem.

6. **Seasons Report** "Stopping by Woods on a Snowy Evening" takes place on "the darkest evening of the year," namely the winter solstice (December 21). This date marks the beginning of winter in the Northern Hemisphere. Research the astronomical definitions of "solstice" and "equinox." Present your results in a brief written report.

7. **Debate** Do you think the city or the countryside offers better subjects and themes for poetry? Together with some of your classmates, stage a debate. Divide into two teams. Remember to support your opinions with persuasive arguments and specific examples. Have the rest of the class vote on which side is more persuasive.

Extension Activities

1. **Story Expansion** Write a paragraph to expand the story. In your paragraph, tell what Grandfather might have done if he had been in the house the night the bed fell. As a springboard for your writing, use what you learn about Grandfather in the second paragraph of the story.

2. **Letter** Suppose that you are Briggs Beall. Write a letter home telling about some of your unusual experiences during your visit to the Thurbers' house. Feel free to expand the story by making up some new incidents, but keep Briggs's character consistent with the way he is portrayed in the story.

3. **Family Tree** The Thurber family seems to have more than its share of unusual or eccentric relatives. Draw a family tree showing the members of the Thurber household together with their amusing or offbeat characteristics. Write a sentence or two about each person you show on the family tree.

4. **Paragraph** Would you like to have the Thurbers as neighbors? In a paragraph, explain why or why not. As you list your reasons, make some specific references to the people and events described in "The Night the Bed Fell."

5. **Contest Poster** Join with a small group of students. Assume that you are the editorial board of a story magazine. Create a poster advertising a contest for humorous stories or essays. On the poster, explain the rules of the contest and identify the prize. Illustrate your poster with an appropriate drawing or design.

6. **Sound Track** Working with a partner or a small group, choose one or more musical selections for the sound track of a film version of "The Night the Bed Fell." If possible, record the music on audiocassette, and then use it as background for a story theater presentation.

7. **Magazine Research** Investigate the *New Yorker* magazine, where James Thurber worked for many years as a writer and illustrator. Find a recent issue of the magazine. Look at the table of contents, and skim the cartoons and reviews. Then sum up your research in a paragraph that profiles the magazine, describing the kind of publication it is.

Unit 4: Resolving Conflicts

Extension Activities

1. **Critical Response** Good science fiction must have a certain basis in fact, or it will not seem believable. In a paragraph, explain whether or not you think this story is realistic. Give reasons to support your opinion.

2. **Anecdote** An anecdote is a brief story told to entertain listeners or to point up a lesson. Write an anecdote about a time when you (or someone you know) were picked on unfairly. If you wish, include your feelings about this event and your reactions to it.

3. **Sequel** What do you think happens when Margot is released from the closet? Do the other children avoid her? Do they apologize? What does Margot say and do? Write a short sequel to the story.

4. **Metaphors** A metaphor makes a direct comparison between two unlike things. For example, in Bradbury's story the sun is called a yellow crayon, and rain is called a tatting drum and a clear bead necklace. Write a fresh, imaginative metaphor of your own for each of the following: sun, rain, thunder, lightning, snow.

5. **Illustration** In the paragraph that begins with "They stopped running and stood in the great jungle that covered Venus, that grew and never stopped growing . . ." Bradbury provides a vividly detailed description of the setting. Working with a small group, use this paragraph as a springboard to create a story illustration showing the setting on Venus.

6. **Author Report** Use Internet resources to find out more about the life and works of Ray Bradbury, who has won many awards. Organize the results of your research into a brief written report.

7. **Science Report** The planet Venus is often visible as either the morning or the evening star. Do some research on the orbit of Venus, its apparent brightness or magnitude compared to other celestial bodies, and the best times to see it in the morning or evening sky during the next few months. Sum up your findings in an oral report to the class as a whole.

Extension Activities

1. **Oral Report** Find out more about cattle drives. Use library or Internet resources to compile information about this job and the people who perform it. Organize your information in a report, and present it to the class.

2. **Letter** Suppose that you are Bess's father, the landlord, in "The Highwayman." After the tragedy, write a letter to the highwayman's mother telling her what happened. In your letter, extend your sympathy, and tell how you feel about the highwayman's activities and the young people's relationship.

3. **Analysis** In which of these two selections does the writer use suspense most effectively? Write a paragraph explaining your choice. In your paragraph, compare and contrast both selections with respect to the use of suspense.

4. **Letter to the Editor** Assume that you are a settler in western Kansas. Use some of the factual details in "The Real Story of a Cowboy's Life" to write a letter to a newspaper editor. In your letter, argue that the quarantine lines for cattle drives should be strictly enforced.

5. **Film Review** Together with a small group, watch one of the classic Hollywood westerns: for example, *My Darling Clementine* (1946), *Red River* (1948), *High Noon* (1952), *Shane* (1953), *Bad Day at Black Rock* (1955), or *The Searchers* (1956). Share your ideas and reactions with your group. Then write a brief evaluation in the form of a film review.

6. **Skit** With a partner or a small group, write a skit involving Teddy Blue and Charles Goodnight. Base your skit on events that might have happened on the trail during a cattle drive. As a springboard for your writing, use the factual information in "The Real Story of a Cowboy's Life." When you have finished writing, rehearse your skit, and then perform it for an audience of classmates.

7. **Ballad in Performance** What kinds of music and dance would be appropriate for a performance of "The Highwayman"? Use Internet or library resources to carry out some research, and then sum up your results in a written report.

"Amigo Brothers" by Piri Thomas
"The Walk" by Thomas Hardy
"Justin Lebo" by Phillip Hoose
"The Rider" by Naomi Shihab Nye

Extension Activities

1. **Letter to the Editor** In "Justin Lebo," you read how a letter to the editor can have dramatic results. What issues or problems do you care about at school or in your community? Choose a topic, and write a letter to the editor of your school or community newspaper giving your views. Suggest a course of action that your readers can take. Support your arguments with reasons, facts, or examples.

2. **Sequel** Write a sequel to "Amigo Brothers." In your sequel, reveal who won the fight between Antonio and Felix. Also describe how this outcome affected their friendship. You might go on to tell how the winner performs in the Golden Gloves Championship Tournament.

3. **Garage Sale Plan** What's involved in organizing a garage sale? Find out by doing some Internet research or by asking knowledgeable friends and neighbors whom you know well. Then write up an organizational plan for holding a successful garage sale.

4. **Personal Symbols** In Naomi Shihab Nye's "The Rider," a bicycle becomes a personal symbol of freedom for the speaker. What or whom would you choose as your own personal symbol of freedom? Write a paragraph explaining your choice.

5. **Music Report** Together with a small group, use the Internet and the library, or interview knowledgeable students to find out more about *salsa* music. If possible, record some *salsa* music on audiocassette. Present your results in an oral report.

6. **Fundraising Survey** What are some of the strategies that people and organizations use to raise funds for various causes? In "Justin Lebo," you read about publicity and matching programs. Together with a small group of classmates, carry out a survey in your community to determine the most frequently used fundraising strategies. Sum up your results in a written report.

7. **Author Report** Thomas Hardy (1840–1928) was one of England's greatest novelists as well as one of its most talented poets. Use Internet or library resources to find out more about Hardy's long career and some of his major works. Sum up your results in an oral report.

Extension Activities

1. **Diary Entry** Assume you are the substitute executive producer. Write a diary entry giving your reactions to the bloopers and blunders made during the newscast. Be sure to comment specifically on how you think Charles Osgood, as the anchor, handled the situation.

2. **Compare and Contrast** Charles Osgood has worked in both radio and television news. Listen to a radio news broadcast, and then watch a television news broadcast on the same day. Write a paragraph in which you compare and contrast the two media. Which medium reports the news more effectively, in your opinion? Why?

3. **Paragraphs** While most news programs are broadcast live, some interviews and background information contained in news reports may be recorded on videotape in advance. Make a list of the advantages and disadvantages of prerecorded events and information. Summarize your thoughts in a paragraph or two.

4. **Bloooper List** Assume that you are the producer of either a television sports or entertainment program that turns out to be as full of bloopers and blunders as Osgood's newscast. Write a list of the kinds of accidents and mishaps that might go wrong on your program. Use Osgood's essay as a springboard.

5. **Oral Report** How often do you find the nightly news to be funny? Research and report on humor in the news. Watch the nightly news on television for three evenings in a row. Take notes on the stories, if any, that appear to be amusing, and note where they appear in the broadcast. Is there a pattern? Why? Present your findings in a brief oral report.

6. **Illustration** Working with a small group, select one of the incidents in Osgood's newscast and draw an illustration of it. Use clues in the text as a springboard.

7. **Media Report** Use Internet or library resources to investigate the history of one of the major news networks: ABC, CBS, CNN, or NBC. Write up your results in a short report.

Extension Activities

1. **Compare and Contrast** Write a paragraph or two in which you compare and contrast cats and dogs as pets. What are the advantages and disadvantages of owning each species? Tell which you would prefer to have as a pet and why.

2. **Personal Choices** Assume that you work as a veterinarian for a zoo. Which animals would you look forward to treating? Which animals would be your *least* favorites? Explain your personal choices in a paragraph.

3. **Poem** Write a short poem about Oscar. Try to use as many images that appeal to the five senses as you can. Your poem may or may not rhyme. When you have finished writing, read your poem aloud to a small audience of classmates, friends, or family members.

4. **Sequel** How does Oscar's life unfold after the story is over? Write a sequel that involves an exciting new adventure for him, or one in which he develops a new personality quirk. You might feature the Gibbons family as well as the Herriots in your sequel, or you might make up some new quirky characters of your own.

5. **Community Resource Report** Every year in many parts of the country, household pets are abandoned by irresponsible owners. Find out about your community's resources for handling these animals. You could interview a veterinarian at an animal shelter or hospital, for example. Write up your results in a brief report.

6. **Book Report** Two best-selling books about pets are by Elizabeth Marshall Thomas: *The Hidden Life of Dogs* (1993) and *The Tribe of Tiger: Cats and Their Culture* (1994). Locate either one of these books in a library and read a chapter of the text. Then write a summary of your reading, and give your evaluation of Thomas's approach. Tell whether or not you would like to read the whole book or would recommend the book to a friend.

7. **TV Film Review** Together with a small group of classmates, watch one of the television films made from James Herriot's stories: *All Creatures Great and Small* (1974), directed by Claude Whatham, or *All Things Bright and Beautiful* (1979), directed by Eric Till. Write a brief review in which you share your evaluation of the film.

"The Luckiest Time of All" by Lucille Clifton
"in Just–" by E. E. Cummings
"The Microscope" by Maxine Kumin
"Sarah Cynthia Sylvia Stout" by Shel Silverstein
"Father William" by Lewis Carroll

Extension Activities

1. **Quirky Dialogue** Write a dialogue between two of your favorite quirky characters in these selections. For example, what would a conversation be like between Father William and Sarah Cynthia Sylvia Stout? Or what might the balloonman in "in Just–" say to Anton Leeuwenhoek?

2. **Paragraph** What qualities or personality traits of inventors might make them seem quirky or eccentric to other people? Write a paragraph in which you state and support your opinion. You may support your speculations by referring to the text of "The Microscope" or by mentioning inventors you know or have read about.

3. **Compare and Contrast** There are many interesting uses of language in these selections: for example, dialect in "The Luckiest Time of All," coined words in "in Just–," amusing rhymes and sound effects in "Sarah Cynthia Sylvia Stout," and formal word choices in "Father William." Write one or two paragraphs in which you compare and contrast the language used in two of the selections in this group.

4. **Hyperbole** Skim recent sports stories or feature stories in newspapers and magazines. Find some examples of hyperbole, or exaggeration for effect. Write a paragraph in which you evaluate the effectiveness of hyperbole as an attention-getting device.

5. **Oral Performance** Choose one of the selections that you think especially lends itself to oral performance. Decide how you can best use facial expressions, gestures, and body postures—in addition to your voice—in an oral performance of this selection. Consider using a tape recorder and a mirror during your rehearsals. When you are satisfied with your rendition, present your performance to a live audience.

6. **Cartoon or Comic Strip** Working with a small group, create a cartoon or comic strip about a quirky character in your community. Maintain a light, amusing, and affectionate tone.

7. **Oral Report** Use Internet or library resources to investigate one of the quirky imaginary characters in Lewis Carroll's classic tales, *Alice's Adventures in Wonderland* and *Through the Looking-Glass*. Prepare an oral report in which you describe the character's appearance, manner of speaking, and personality traits.

"Zoo" by Edward D. Hoch
"The Hippopotamus" by Ogden Nash
"How the Snake Got Poison" by Zora Neale Hurston

Extension Activities

1. **Letter** Imagine that Professor Hugo has just visited your community with either the Kaanians or another strange-looking set of creatures. Write a letter to a friend in which you share your reactions to the exhibit. Also describe the way in which people in your community behave in regard to the exhibit.

2. **Paragraph** A serious point or practical lesson often lies beneath the surface of a humorous poem or story. Choose one of the selections in this group, and write a paragraph giving your interpretation of the theme, or overall message, of the selection. Support your opinion with specific quotations from the text.

3. **Humorous Dialogue** Write a humorous dialogue in which a number of animals share their thoughts on the subject of human beings. For example, you might include a hippopotamus and a rattlesnake in your script.

4. **Story Notes** Do some research on one of the following animals with unusual names: kodkod, tarantula, zorilla, aye-aye, or bongo. Find out which family the animal belongs to, as well as details about its appearance, geographical distribution, habitat, and behavior. Then write notes for a humorous story that features this animal as a major character.

5. **Oral Performance** Choose one of these selections and develop an oral performance of it for a live audience. Use body language, facial expressions, and gestures to enhance the humor of the text.

6. **Illustration** Working with a small group, choose one of these selections and develop an illustration for the text. Don't forget to quote an appropriate line or phrase from the text as a caption for your illustration.

7. **Report** Using Internet or library resources, explore recent scientific research in the field of animal cognition. Do animals think? What means do they use to communicate? Can they make decisions or feel emotions, or are they simply creatures of instinct? Write up your findings in a brief report.

Extension Activities

1. **Paragraph** Suspense is the quality of a story that makes the reader or the audience tense and uncertain about the outcome. Write a paragraph explaining how O. Henry creates suspense in "After Twenty Years."

2. **Dialogue** Write the dialogue between Jimmy Wells and the plainclothes officer that takes place before the arrest. Use clues in the story as a springboard for your dialogue.

3. **Interview** In addition to arresting those who break the law, how do law enforcement officers help your community? To find out, interview a police officer, a journalist, a career advisor, or someone in the health professions. Summarize your results in a short oral report.

4. **Story** Write a brief summary of an alternative version of O. Henry's story. Suppose that Bob had recognized Jimmy Wells first, instead of the other way around. How would he have handled his sudden realization that his old friend was now a police officer? Read your new version to an audience of classmates or friends who are familiar with the original. Do they prefer your version to O. Henry's?

5. **Explanation** Is there anyone with whom you would make an agreement similar to the one made between Bob and Jimmy? Write a paragraph explaining your reasons for promising to meet that person in a certain place exactly twenty years from now.

6. **Performance and Discussion** Rehearse an oral performance of the story for an audience of younger students. In your performance, use gestures and facial expressions, and try to alter your voice in order to present the different characters effectively. After you tell the story, invite members of the audience to discuss their reactions to the tale.

7. **Research Report** Use library or online resources to find out more about the adventuresome life and the writing career of O. Henry (William Sydney Porter). Sum up your results in a brief oral report.

Extension Activities

1. **Mottoes** Kipling says that the motto of the whole family of mongooses is "Run and find out." Working in a small group, choose three favorite species of animals or birds and make up a motto for each. Just as Kipling's motto stresses the mongoose's curiosity, your mottoes should point to an important physical feature or behavior trait of each species. If you wish, choose one or two special favorites and draw an illustration, using your motto as the caption.

2. **Snake Report** Kipling mentions the cobra and the krait, two of the most important poisonous snakes in India. What are the major species of poisonous snakes in the United States? What do these snakes look like and where do they live? Do some research to find out, and then summarize your results in a short written report.

3. **Field Guide Entry** Choose one of the following species mentioned in the story and research its appearance, diet, behavior, and habitat (where the species lives): cobra, krait, mongoose, tailorbird, coppersmith, muskrat. Write a short field guide entry to summarize the information you discover.

4. **Diary Entries** Write three or four diary entries from the point of view of Teddy's father, describing his reactions to the different events in the story. For example, you might describe the father's reaction to Rikki-tikki's arrival.

5. **News Feature** Rudyard Kipling was born in Bombay, India. These days, Bombay is sometimes nicknamed "Bollywood." More Indian films are produced there every year than are made in Hollywood. Working with a small group, do some research on the Indian film industry. What kinds of movies are most popular? How are film stars regarded in India? When you have finished your research, write up the results in the form of a two-minute feature for a radio or television newscast.

6. **Report** Kipling mentions the Hindu god Brahma. Use Internet and library reources to find out more about some or all of these major divinities of Hinduism: Shiva, Vishnu, Kali, Durga, Ganesh, and Hanuman. How are these gods and goddesses depicted in art and sculpture? Sum up your findings in a written report.

7. **Round Table Discussion** Ricki-tikki-tavi is one of the most popular short stories ever written in English. One of the secrets of its appeal is the way Kipling makes a hero out of the little mongoose. What specific heroic qualities does Rikki have? Together with a small group of classmates, hold a round table discussion in which you share ideas about Rikki's personality traits.

Extension Activities

1. **Diary Entries** Suppose that you are Harry and that you are keeping a diary during the period covered in "Papa's Parrot." Write four or five diary entries in which you express your feelings about your father, your friends, and Rocky.

2. **Illustration** Working with a small group, choose a scene from "Papa's Parrot" that you think lends itself especially well to illustration. Create a drawing or painting of this scene. Then choose an appropriate phrase or line of dialogue from the story to use as a caption for your illustration.

3. **Research Report** Some parrots have been trained to an amazing degree and possess a large vocabulary. Use Internet or library resources to find out about these birds. What is the latest thinking among scientists about parrots' intelligence? Sum up your results in a brief research report.

4. **Dialogue** Write a dialogue between Harry and his father. In your dialogue, explore Harry's feelings about his realization that his father misses his visits to the store.

5. **On the Air** Radio and television often use musical "jingles" to make an announcement to listeners. Write a jingle to advertise the candy store. As you create your jingle, be sure to determine the audience you are trying to reach, the tone you want to set with the jingle, and phrases you want to include.

6. **Interview** What are some of the emergency procedures used in hospitals or by emergency service personnel for victims of heart attack? Working with a partner, interview someone in the health professions to find out. Sum up your results in an oral report.

7. **Paragraph** What did you enjoy most about the story? Write a paragraph stating your opinion, and then support your choice with reasons, examples, and specific references to the story.

Extension Activities

1. **Diary** Imagine that you are Suzy, and write the next entry in your diary. Write about your developing friendship with Leah.

2. **Research Report** Use Internet or library resources to find out about the exhibits at the United States Holocaust Memorial Museum, located in Washington, D.C. Present your results in the form of an oral report to the class as a whole.

3. **Research** Use library and Internet resources to find out more about refugee camps around the world. Write a short summary of your findings.

4. **Letter** Suppose that it is now ten or fifteen years after the events described in "Suzy and Leah." Write a letter from Suzy to Leah or from Leah to Suzy. Are the two young women still friends? What is their perspective on the events of 1944? Use the story as a springboard for your writing.

5. **Film Review** There have been many films made about WWII and the plight of the concentration camp victims. Together with a small group of classmates, use Internet or library resources to identify some of these films. Choose one of the films to watch, then evaluate it in a brief written review.

6. **Paragraph** Leah and Suzy change their opinions of each other. Think of a time when you suddenly realized that your first impressions about another person were unfair or inaccurate. Write a paragraph about a situation in which you changed your mind about another person.

7. **Round Table Discussion** What practical benefits come from keeping a diary? Together with a small group of classmates, hold a round table discussion in which you share ideas about keeping a regular diary. If you wish, ask some adults to join your round table, and invite them to contribute their perspective on diary writing.

"Ribbons" by Laurence Yep
"The Treasure of Lemon Brown" by Walter Dean Myers

Extension Activities

1. **Paragraph** How are Greg and Stacy alike? How are they different? Write a paragraph comparing and contrasting the two characters. At the conclusion of your paragraph, tell which character you would like better as a friend, and explain your choice.

2. **Report** What is ballet practice like? What physical and mental skills does a person use? Interview someone who is involved in ballet, or use library or Internet resources to find out more about this art. Summarize your results in a brief written report.

3. **Letter** Write a letter that Greg might give or send to his father. Assume that Greg has a change of heart and decides to tell his father about his experience with Lemon Brown. However, Greg thinks it is better to write his story down in a letter rather than tell it face to face.

4. **Report** Use library or Internet resources to investigate some aspect of the visual or performing arts of China, such as painting, sculpture, architecture, music, or dance. Summarize your results in an illustrated oral report.

5. **Advertisement** Working with a small group, choose one of the two stories in this pair. Assume that the story will be made into an hour-long dramatization for television. With your group, design a magazine or newspaper advertisement for the television program.

6. **Newspaper Feature** "The Treasure of Lemon Brown" takes place in Harlem, a largely African American neighborhood in New York City with a fascinating history. Do some research about the poets, musicians, and artists who lived in Harlem during the Harlem Renaissance of the 1920s and 1930s. Then write a brief newspaper feature telling readers some of your results.

7. **Illustration** Working with a partner, trade ideas about which story in this pair you prefer. Then choose your favorite scene in this story for illustration. When you have finished drawing the scene, choose an appropriate phrase or line of dialogue from the story that can serve as a caption.

Extension Activities

1. **Map** Draw a map of the neighborhood depicted in "Stolen Day." Be sure to include places mentioned such as the school, the pond, and the spring. You may want to make a scale for your map to show how far the landmarks are from one another.

2. **Humorous Narrative** In "Stolen Day," Anderson tells a humorous story about the day he decided to fake an illness to take off from school. Try to remember a funny incident that happened to your own or a friend's family. Write a short narrative describing the incident. Keep the style relaxed, conversational, and humorous. Share your narrative with the class.

3. **List of Titles** Why do you think Sherwood Anderson chose to name this story "Stolen Day"? Make a list of other titles that might be appropriate. Next to each title, write a few sentences explaining why that title suits the story.

4. **Paragraph** What would you do in the course of a single stolen day? Would you spend the day alone or with friends? What time of year would it be, and what activities would you choose? Write a paragraph telling how you would spend this precious time.

5. **Readers Theater** Together with a small group, organize a readers theater presentation of "Stolen Day." First, go over the story carefully to assign parts. You may want to use the narrative as a springboard to increase the amount of dialogue for some of the characters. If your group wishes, two or three students can share the task of reading the narrator's part.

6. **Picture This** Choose four to eight scenes from the story that you can clearly envision. Create a poster describing the scenes you choose, and illustrate them with original art or computer images.

7. **Skit** Use the ending of the story to create a skit showing the reaction of the boy's family to his revelation that he thinks he has a terrible disease and could not spend the full day in school because of it. Keep in mind that he knows his revelation will not be easily lived down, and depict at least one future scene in your skit.

Extension Activities

1. **Paragraph** "How to Enjoy Poetry" is an expository essay divided into a number of sections. Look back at the titles of these sections. Then write a paragraph addressed to the author. In your paragraph, tell which section of the essay you think is most interesting, and why.

2. **Poem** Choose a photograph of a family member or friend and study it closely. Then write a poem in which you portray the personality of this person. Also include in your poem the emotions that the photograph inspires in you.

3. **Mythology Report** Orion and Croesus are famous people from ancient Greek mythology. Using a dictionary or encyclopedia, find out more about one of these figures. Sum up your results in a brief written report.

4. **Notes for a Poem** Dickey mentions some everyday objects that might make good subjects for poetry, such as an ice cube, a rock, and a leaf. Make a list of five ordinary objects. Beside each one, make notes on one or two images that you associate with the object. After you have finished your notes, choose one object out of the five that you think would be the best focus for a short poem.

5. **Literature Report** Two writers of world literature whom James Dickey mentions are Dante and Aldous Huxley. Use library or Internet resources to find out more about one of these writers. Summarize your results in an oral report to the class.

6. **Rhymes** All poetry does not need to rhyme, but rhyme is a musical device that is pleasing in itself and helps you to remember a poem. In the library, locate a rhyming dictionary. Scan the pages and look for rhymes that strike you as especially clever or interesting. Copy down some unusual rhymes, and then share them with a small group of classmates.

7. **Poster** Design a poster for a poetry contest or "slam." Use some of James Dickey's arguments in the selection as a springboard for your poster. When you have finished work, get together with a small group of classmates and display your posters in an exhibit.

Extension Activities

1. **Comparison and Contrast** Write a paragraph in which you compare and contrast the young Russell Baker with his sister Doris. What similarities and differences between the children do you find? Which one would you prefer to have known in school?

2. **Dialogue** Write a dialogue that the young Annie Dillard might have had with Mikey Fahey after the man who chased them returned to his car. Use the events and characterization in Dillard's essay as a springboard for your dialogue.

3. **Maxims** Russell Baker's mother is fond of quoting maxims, or wise sayings, such as "If at first you don't succeed, try, try again." Is anyone in your family fond of maxims? Use your own experience or consult a dictionary of proverbs in the library to write a list of five proverbs that you think contain especially valuable wisdom or advice.

4. **Paragraph** Russell was not a good salesperson, but his sister Doris was. In a paragraph, explain the qualities that you think a good salesperson needs. At the end of your paragraph, explain whether or not you think you would be a good salesperson.

5. **Magazine Poster** Working with a partner, locate some old issues of the *Saturday Evening Post* in your school or community library. Flip through the pages to get an idea of what this magazine was like. Then design a poster advertising the magazine and inviting the public to subscribe to it.

6. **Story Theater** Together with a group of classmates, organize a readers theater presentation of Russell Baker's autobiographical essay "No Gumption." If you wish, several students can take turns presenting the part of the narrator.

7. **Sound Track** You are directing a half-hour television version of Annie Dillard's "The Chase." Choose a piece of music that would be suitable for the sound track during the chase itself. In a few sentences, explain why you chose this particular music.

Extension Activities

1. **News Article** In his biographical essay on Nolan Ryan, William W. Lace stresses the baseball pitcher's concern with a healthful diet. Use health texts, encyclopedias, or Internet resources to find out about the Food Pyramid. Research the different food groups and the recommended daily amounts of each. Summarize your findings in a news article.

2. **Interview Notes** Assume that you can interview Nolan Ryan. Using the biographical information you have read about him as a springboard, write a list of questions you would like to ask.

3. **History Research** The Texas Rangers baseball team is named for a famous law enforcement organization, the Texas Rangers. Use library resources or the Internet to carry out some research about the history and traditions of this group. Present your results in an oral report to the class.

4. **Advice Column** What are the three most important character or personality traits that help a person to achieve excellence in his or her chosen field? Write an advice column in which you give your opinion. Be sure to support your view with reasons.

5. **Book Jacket** Working with two other classmates, design a book jacket for Nolan Ryan's biography. Specify a photograph or illustration that will appear on the cover. Write the "blurb" for the book jacket that will interest bookstore browsers and compel them to buy the book and read it.

6. **Letter to the Editor** Write a letter to the editor of your school newspaper. In your letter, recommend someone you admire as the next graduation speaker for your school. Explain how the record of achievement or excellence of this person might serve as an inspiration to you and your classmates.

7. **Interview** Imagine that Nolan Ryan is coming to your school, and that you have been chosen to interview him for the school paper. Write a list of questions that you would like to ask him, then brainstorm his answers to at least three of the questions. Keep in mind that your audience has a variety of interests; not everyone knows a great deal about baseball.

from *Barrio Boy* by Ernesto Galarza
"**I Am a Native of North America**" by Chief Dan George
"**Rattlesnake Hunt**" by Marjorie Kinnan Rawlings
"**All Together Now**" by Barbara Jordan

Extension Activities

1. **Fact Sheet** Choose one of the four essays in this group of selections. What did you learn from this essay? Reread the essay carefully, and write a list of facts that you did not know before. When you have finished, exchange papers with a classmate and discuss the factual information that each of you listed.

2. **Talent Day Program** In Ernesto Galarza's class at the Lincoln School, many of the students had different talents. Join with a group of your classmates and plan a Talent Day celebration in order to showcase students' various talents and cultural backgrounds. Create a program or brochure for Talent Day, illustrating it with suitable art.

3. **Report** "Rattlesnake Hunt" is set in a unique area of southern Florida called the Everglades. Since 1947, much of this area has been protected as a national park. Use library or Internet resources to learn more about the landforms and wildlife that make the Everglades a precious national treasure. Sum up your findings in an oral report to the class.

4. **Poem** Using either "I am a Native of North America" or "All Together Now" as a springboard, write a poem about the power or importance of caring for another person. In your poem, be sure to include some vivid imagery that appeals to one or more of the five senses. Your poem may or may not rhyme.

5. **Brochure** Use history books, encyclopedias, and Internet resources to assemble a brochure about Ellis Island, which served as the chief entry station for millions of immigrants to the United States between 1892 and 1943. From which countries did the immigrants come? Where did they settle? How did they make their living?

6. **Illustration Notes** Join with three or four other classmates. Decide which of the four essays lends itself best to illustration. Then make some notes on how you would illustrate various passages from the essay. In your notes, indicate the medium you think would work best: for example, watercolors, cartoons, or collages.

7. **Round Table Discussion** Miss Hopley's posture made a powerful impression on the young Ernesto Galarza. How important is posture in the impressions that people make on others? Join with a small group of classmates, and share your views in a round table discussion.

*A **Christmas Carol** Act I* by Charles Dickens
dramatized by Israel Horovitz

Extension Activities

1. **Adjective Lists** Early in Act I, Scrooge is described as a "squeezing, wrenching, grasping, scraping, clutching, covetous, old sinner." Choose three other characters from this play or a trio of characters from another story or play that you have enjoyed. Write a similarly colorful list of adjectives for each character.

2. **Pen Name** Early in his career, Dickens wrote under the pen name "Boz." What pen names might appeal to you if you were a professional writer? Make up a list of three or four possibilities. In a paragraph, explain why you chose these particular pen names.

3. **Resource Survey** The Thin Man and the Portly Man ask Scrooge for a contribution to help the neediest at Christmas time. What organizations exist in your community to help the neediest or to aid the homeless? Carry out a survey by consulting telephone directories and interviewing adults at school or at institutions such as hospitals and community centers. Write up your results in a paragraph or two.

4. **Round Table Discussion** Get together with a few classmates and discuss the role of sound effects in Act I of the play. How do the sound effects enhance the action? What preparations would you make in order to produce these sound effects, or similar ones, for a live performance?

5. **Analysis** How does Dickens establish and maintain suspense in Act I? Write a paragraph or two in which you discuss the techniques the author uses in order to keep you uncertain about what will happen next.

6. **Illustration** Join with a small group of classmates and select a scene in Act I that you think lends itself especially well to illustration. Create a drawing, painting, or collage to illustrate this scene, and give your art work a caption drawn from the text.

7. **Research Report** Use Internet or library resources to explore what London was like in 1843, the year *A Christmas Carol* takes place. What were some of the landmarks of the city? How did people get around and do their shopping? In what sort of houses did they live and how did they dress? Where did they go to buy copies of stories like "A Christmas Carol"? Write up your results in a brief report.

© Prentice-Hall, Inc.

Unit 8: Drama

Extension Activities

1. **Holiday Foods** The stage directions in Act II, Scene 1, provide a long list of foods traditionally associated with an English Christmas. Choose another holiday that you connect with special foods. Write a paragraph in which you list these holiday treats.

2. **Prediction** Do you think Scrooge's change for the better will be permanent, or will he go back to his old ways? Write a paragraph in which you state your view and support it with quotations from the text of the play.

3. **Dialogue** As you learned in the "Guide for Reading" in your textbook, Dickens had a difficult childhood. Use the information given in the text as a springboard to write an imaginary dialogue between two members of the Dickens family during the time that Charles was a teenager.

4. **Diary Entry** Assume you are Bob Cratchit. It is the day after Christmas. Write a diary entry in which you record your reactions to Scrooge's change of heart.

5. **Review** Join with a small group and watch the television adaptation of "A Christmas Carol" directed by Clive Donner and starring George C. Scott as Scrooge (1984). Then write a brief review in which you evaluate the film for its presentation of several specific dramatic elements. Among the elements on which you might want to focus are some of the following: acting, costumes, sets, special effects, dialogue, and music.

6. **Dialogue and Performance** With two classmates, write a humorous dialogue in which the three ghosts discuss their experiences with Scrooge. Think of how the ghosts would have felt as they showed Scrooge each incident and watched his reaction. Practice and perform your dialogue for the rest of the class.

7. **Letter to Marley** Imagine that you are Scrooge. Jacob Marley has asked you which of the ghosts had the strongest impact on you. Jot down the names of each ghost. Under each name list what the ghost showed you and the effect it had on you. Decide which ghost was most responsible for changing your behavior. Write a letter to Marley telling which ghost you chose and why.

Extension Activities

1. **Poster** "The Monsters Are Due on Maple Street" takes place in a small town. Design a poster of small town scenes. Include illustrations or photographs of some of the details described in the screenplay. For example, show houses with front porches, a man polishing his car parked in front of his house, a Good Humor man selling ice cream to children, and neighbors watering their lawn and chatting to each other over their fences.

2. **Diary Entry** Imagine that you are Tommy. Choose a specific moment in the play, and write a diary entry giving your feelings about the way the adults on Maple Street are behaving. Also predict how the action will turn out.

3. **Crisis Summary** In "The Monsters Are Due on Maple Street," an unusual event turns neighbor against neighbor. Write a paragraph about how some future natural disaster, such as a hurricane or flood, might threaten to divide your community or might even bring it together.

4. **Editorial** Imagine that you are the editor of a weekly newspaper read by the residents of Maple Street. Write an editorial expressing your opinion about the lessons to be drawn from the day the monsters were due to arrive. Support your opinion with specific references to the play.

5. **Research Report** Use Internet or library resources to do some research about the early days of television in the 1950s. What kinds of shows did television feature? How many people owned television sets in 1955? Sum up your results in a brief report.

6. **Photo Essay** The play mentions several astronomical phenomena, such as meteors, a nebula, and sunspots. Together with a small group, do a photo essay on a topic in astronomy, using interesting facts or statistics as captions for your photos.

7. **Social Studies Report** Using Internet or library resources, research the protection of free speech under the First Amendment to the Constitution. What kinds of censorship of the press or of entertainment programs in the media are allowed under the First Amendment? Sum up your findings in a brief report.

Unit 8: Drama

"The Cremation of Sam McGee" by Robert Service
"Washed in Silver" by James Stephens
"Winter" by Nikki Giovanni

Extension Activities

1. **Letter** Assume you are the speaker in "The Cremation of Sam McGee." Write a letter in which you extend your sympathy to Sam's family in Tennessee.

2. **Poem** Using Nikki Giovanni's poem "Winter" as a model, write a short poem of your own that focuses on another season: spring, summer, or fall. In your poem, try to use vivid images that appeal to one or more of the five senses.

3. **Analysis** Three ways in which Robert Service creates humor in this poem are the use of unexpected rhymes, the description of outlandish situations, and the use of colloquial expressions. In a paragraph or two, analyze Service's use of *two* of these techniques, citing specific examples.

4. **Vivid Verbs** In "Washed in Silver," James Stephens uses a group of especially vivid words: *gleaming, blazing, spills, drives, clad,* and *march.* In a paragraph, discuss the ways in which such words make the poem more vivid and appealing. You might compare and contrast some of the words with less colorful synonyms that would have been less effective: for example, *gleaming* versus *shining,* or *spills* versus *shows.*

5. **Oral Performance** Rehearse "The Cremation of Sam McGee" for an oral performance. If you wish, work with a small group and divide the stanzas among the members. Or you might design a reading so that certain parts of the poem are performed by individuals and other parts by a chorus of the entire group.

6. **Wildlife Report** How do the plants and animals of the Far North adapt to the extreme conditions of the climate? Do some library research to find out, and then summarize your findings in a paragraph or two.

7. **Photo Essay** Consider the activities and feelings that you associate with a particular season of the year in your community. Then develop a photo essay that presents a cross section of activities linked with the season. Use the images and captions in your photo essay to express or suggest your own emotions about the season.

Extension Activities

1. **Concrete Poem** Choose an animal and write a short concrete poem about it. In your poem, be sure to refer to the animal's physical appearance, and mention some of its most striking habits. Use language that appeals to one or more of the five senses.

2. **Journal Entry** Imagine that earlier today you spent an hour or so with the speaker of "The Pasture." Write a journal entry in which you tell about the chores that you completed. Also discuss your impressions of the speaker and the setting.

3. **Research Report** Seals and sea lions make up a group of mammals called the pinnipeds. There are thirty-three different species in this group, widely distributed all over the world. Use Internet or library resources to find out more about the remarkable adaptations of these animals to aquatic life.

4. **Analysis** An important element in each of the three haiku by Bashō is the speaker's sudden perception of a contrast. In a paragraph, analyze the function of contrast in each of these short poems.

5. **Author Report** Use library or Internet resources to find out more about Robert Frost's distinguished career as a poet. For example, you might research the works for which he won the Pulitzer Prize four times, or you might learn about his appearance at the inauguration of President John F. Kennedy in January 1961. Sum up your findings in a brief written report.

6. **Musical Haiku** Working in a small group, develop a musical version of a haiku. Choose a specific instrument, such as a piano, a guitar, or a recorder. Then experiment with three groups of notes or chords divided into the same pattern as the syllables in a haiku: 5-7-5. Develop your musical haiku so that it suggests a specific image or a certain mood or atmosphere.

7. **Illustration** Join with a small group of classmates. Choose the poem in this group that you think best lends itself to visual illustration. Then develop a drawing, painting, or collage to accompany the poem of your choice.

Extension Activities

1. **Letter** Write a letter to Raymond Richard Patterson. In your letter, tell the author what you learned from his poem about Dr. Martin Luther King, Jr.

2. **Analysis** How does Edgar Allan Poe create a sad, almost tragic mood in his poem "Annabel Lee"? Write a paragraph in which you explore the ways in which the poet uses images and sound effects to create this mood.

3. **Creating a Character** Some experts think that Annabel Lee was not a single historical person but rather a composite figure, a combination of women Poe admired in real life. Writers often combine several people from real life in order to create imaginary but believable characters. Assume that you are creating a character for a poem, story, or play. Which people from real life would you combine into a fictional character? Explain your choices in a paragraph or two.

4. **Personal Interpretation** Poetry is not just something you find in old books or literary magazines. Popular song lyrics—whether or not they rhyme—can be considered poetry. Think about what poetry means to you. Choose your own personal definition of poetry, and write a poem describing your definition. You may use any poetry style you like.

5. **Poetry Advertisement** Design an advertisement in poster form for a poetry reading about "people we have loved and lost." The reading will feature "Martin Luther King," and "Annabel Lee." Use quotations that contain images from these poems in your advertisement.

6. **Respond to a Speech** Dr. Martin Luther King, Jr., was a master of oratory or public speaking. Read his famous speech "I Have a Dream," which was delivered at the March on Washington in August 1963. If possible, listen to a recording of the speech. Then write a paragraph in which you share your reactions.

7. **Poster** Imagine that Poe's poem "Annabel Lee" is the basis for a film or stage adaptation with a plot that focuses on the speaker's doomed love. Working with a small group, design a poster to advertise the premiere of this dramatic work.

Extension Activities

1. **Analysis** Find three examples of alliteration in "Full Fathom Five." Write a paragraph in which you discuss Shakespeare's use of this sound device in the song.

2. **Poem** Write a short poem about an activity that your family or friends enjoy together. If you wish, include a few foreign words to indicate your ethnic heritage in the way Pat Mora does in "Maestro."

3. **Units of Measurement** Using a dictionary, investigate the meaning of the following units of measurement: *fathom, league, furlong, jeroboam,* and *hogshead.* Write up your results in a paragraph.

4. **Alliterative Nicknames** Many famous people have had alliterative nicknames. For example, the baseball player Babe Ruth was called "the Sultan of Swat." Working with a small group, make a list of famous sports figures, actors, authors, or others. Then create some alliterative nicknames for them. Make your nicknames as imaginative and humorous as you can.

5. **Ad Scrapbook** Skim through recent issues of newspapers and magazines, and keep an eye out for clever advertising messages on posters and billboards. Look for examples of alliteration and onomatopoeia. Then work with a small group of classmates to compile a scrapbook of ads that use clever verbal devices.

6. **Song Anthology** "Full Fathom Five" is only one of many famous songs from Shakespeare's plays. Use library or Internet resources to research the text of some of Shakespeare's songs, and also try to discover some musical settings for these pieces. Combine your results in a song anthology.

7. **Career Report** Despite the impressive achievements of modern science, life in the ocean depths remains mysterious in many ways. Use library or Internet resources to investigate careers and technological advances in the field of marine biology. Summarize your findings in a brief report.

Unit 9: Poetry

"The Village Blacksmith" by Henry Wadsworth Longfellow
"Fog" by Carl Sandburg
"Loo-Wit" by Wendy Rose
"Life" by Naomi Long Madgett

Extension Activities

1. **Similes** Write a paragraph in which you identify and discuss two similes from "The Village Blacksmith." Which comparison do you think is the most striking and thought-provoking? Give reasons for your choice.

2. **Humorous Dialogue** Write a humorous dialogue between two personified natural forces: for example, a thunderstorm and a tornado, or a hurricane and a volcano. Give your characters descriptive names.

3. **Analysis** In a paragraph, explore the extended metaphor that Carl Sandburg uses in "Fog." What similarities between the behavior of fog and a cat make this figure of speech especially effective?

4. **Figures of Speech** Figures of speech can be as effective in prose as they are in poetry. Find a newspaper or magazine article that interests you in the field of sports, fashion, or entertainment. Read the article carefully, and make a list of the figures of speech the writer uses.

5. **Interview** Blacksmiths are artists and craftspeople. Interview an artist or craftsperson whom you know to find out what influences his or her work. Write the results of your interview in a paragraph or two.

6. **Pantomime** Try to express some of the actions described in "Loo-Wit" as a pantomime, using only postures, gestures, and facial expressions. Rehearse your performance in front of a mirror or together with a friend or family member. Then present your pantomime to a group of invited guests. Encourage them to follow along in the text of the poem as they watch your performance.

7. **Cliché Watch** In order to be effective, figures of speech have to be fresh and imaginative. Some familiar expressions, however, are so overworked that they have lost their force and become clichés: for example, "fit as a fiddle," "light as a feather," or "heavy as a ton of bricks." Together with a small group, organize a round table discussion in which you identify some familiar clichés. Challenge each other to rework each expression so that it becomes fresher and more striking.

Extension Activities

1. **Letter to the Editor** Write a letter to the editor in which you give your opinion about the king's decisions regarding his daughter's future and the enemy threat. Support your view with facts, reasons, and examples as persuasively as you can.

2. **Paragraph** Write a paragraph in which you discuss the role of one of the following emotions in the legend: jealousy, loyalty, pride, fear, or selfishness.

3. **Research Report** Using Internet or library resources, investigate recent archaeological discoveries about the Aztecs and their culture. Write up your findings in a brief research report.

4. **Evaluation** "Poetic justice" is a term used to describe the outcome of a story or play in which good is rewarded and evil is punished, often in an especially fitting way. Write an evaluation of this legend from the point of view of poetic justice. How does the story illustrate poetic justice, in your opinion? Support your opinion with specific references to the text.

5. **Film Proposal** Would this legend furnish appealing material for a film or a made-for-TV movie? Write a proposal in which you discuss the different elements of the legend, such as character, setting, and plot. Evaluate how effective a visual adaptation of the material might be.

6. **Volcano Timeline** Research some of the most famous volcanic eruptions in history. Create a timeline on which you show the name of the volcano, the date and place of the eruptions, and the numbers of casualties and the nature of the other damage.

7. **History Report** Research the Spanish conquest of Mexico in the sixteenth century, focusing especially on the explorer Hernando Cortés and the last Aztec emperor, Montezuma II. Sum up your findings in a brief written report.

Unit 10: Myths, Legends, and Folk Tales

"The People Could Fly" by Virginia Hamilton
"All Stories Are Anansi's" by Harold Courlander
"The Lion and the Statue" by Aesop
"The Fox and the Crow" by Aesop

Extension Activities

1. **Description** Imagine that you are hearing a storyteller give an oral performance of "The People Could Fly." In a paragraph, describe the setting and the circumstances. Tell about the techniques that a good storyteller might use to hold the attention of a live audience. Use clues in the folk tale as a springboard for your description.

2. **Pantomime Performance** Mime, or act out without words, the story of "The Fox and the Crow." You may take on both roles yourself or work with a classmate. Practice and then perform for a few classmates. Have them give you feedback, and then perform for the whole class.

3. **Sculpture Description** What kind of statue or sculpture do you think lions might make of a typical human? Write a paragraph in which you describe such an imaginary statue.

4. **Analysis** A symbol is a person, a place, an event, or a sign that stands for or represents itself and also something other than itself. For example, a flag often serves as a symbol for a nation or country. Choose a character, an object, or an event from one of these folk tales that functions as a symbol. Write a paragraph in which you explain the layers of meaning that the symbol conveys.

5. **Photo Essay** Join with a small group of classmates. Choose one of the cultures represented in this group of selections, and then develop a photo essay about this culture. Use photos in magazines that you can cut up, and photocopy photos from books. Be sure to write captions for your sequence of images.

6. **Story Theater** Choose one of these folk tales and rehearse the story for an oral performance. In your presentation, try to make gestures, postures, and facial expressions—as well as your tone of voice—contribute to the telling of the story.

7. **Evaluation** Which one of these folk tales would lend itself best to an adaptation as a ballet in which the story is told entirely through music and dance? Write an evaluation in which you discuss your choice for a ballet version. Be sure to support your opinion with specific references to the text.

"Phaëthon, Son of Apollo" by Olivia E. Coolidge
"Demeter and Persephone" by Anne Terry White
"Icarus and Daedalus" by Josephine Preston Peabody

Extension Activities

1. **Personal Response** Which of the three myths in this collection is your favorite? Write a paragraph explaining your choice. Cite examples from the text to support your opinion.

2. **Cartoon Strip** "Phaëthon, Son of Apollo" is an exciting story that uses a lot of visual detail. Work with a group of students to create a cartoon strip that tells the story. Each person can be responsible for a particular image or part of the story. Share your finished cartoon strip with the class.

3. **Dialogue** Write an imaginary dialogue between the god Apollo and the inventor Daedalus about the behavior of their respective sons, Phaëthon and Icarus.

4. **Myth Research** Choose one of the following characters in Greek mythology: Hermes, Aphrodite, Hera, Poseidon, or King Minos of Crete. Using Internet or library resources, investigate some of the mythical tales associated with the figure you choose. Then sum up your results in a brief report.

5. **Modern-day Myth** The lessons that some myths teach still seem relevant today. Two such lessons are "Don't be boastful" and "Don't be stubborn and foolhardy." Write a modern-day myth that teaches a lesson on current events and issues. You may wish to use Greek gods and update their images. Perform your modern-day myth for your class.

6. **Debate** In "Phaëthon, Son of Apollo" and "Daedalus and Icarus," we see a conflict between youthful enthusiasm and prudent experience, or between all-out striving for achievement versus restraint and moderation. Organize a debate in which you take opposing sides on this generational conflict. See how many arguments or examples you can develop to support each side of the question.

7. **Myth Summary** Explore a collection, or anthology, of tales from Greek mythology. Find a tale whose characters, setting, plot, or underlying message particularly interests you. Write a summary of this myth, and then give an oral reading of your summary for an audience of classmates, friends, or family members.